UNDERGROUND

R
I
V
E
R
S

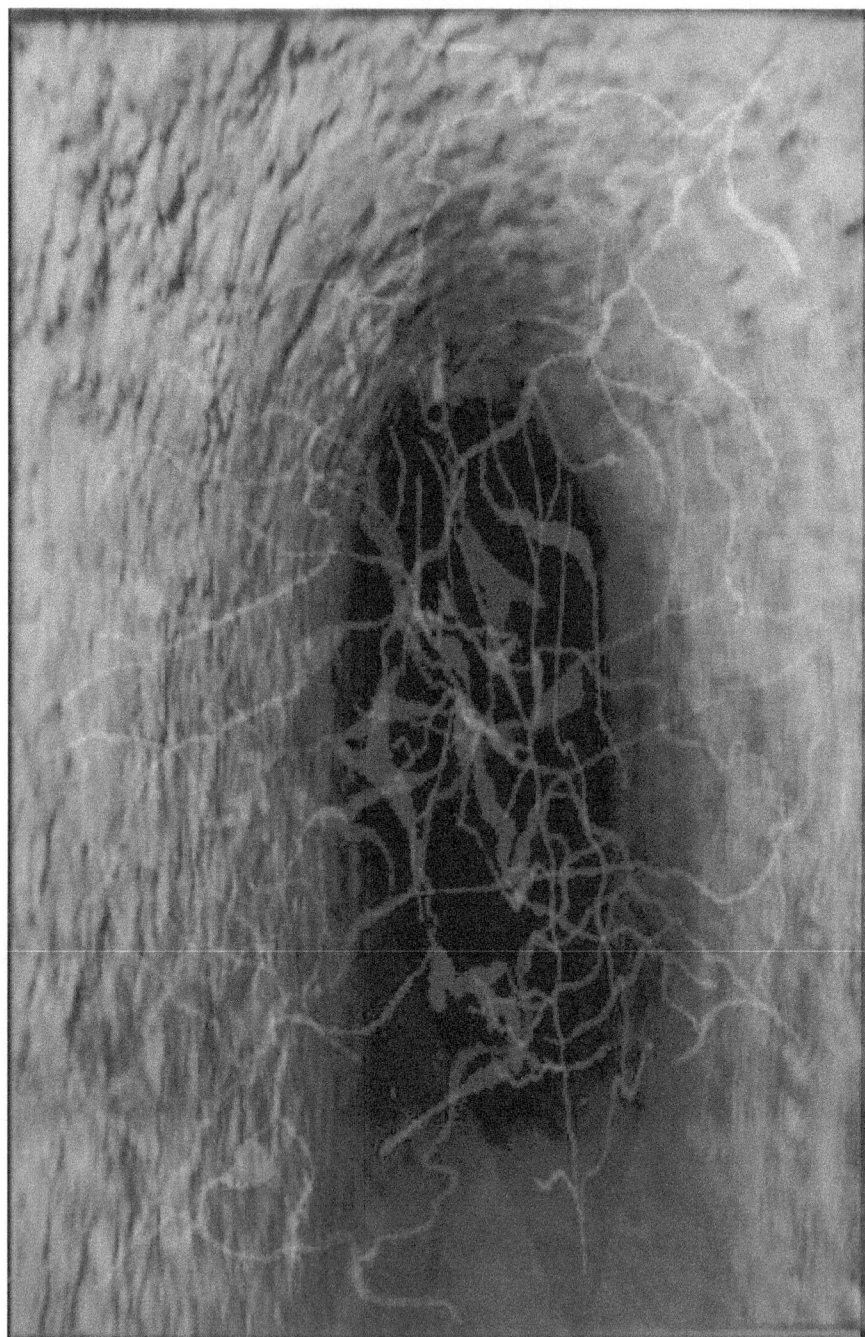

To souls, it is death to become water
& for water death to become earth.
From earth comes water, & from water soul.

-Heraclitus, *Fragment 36*

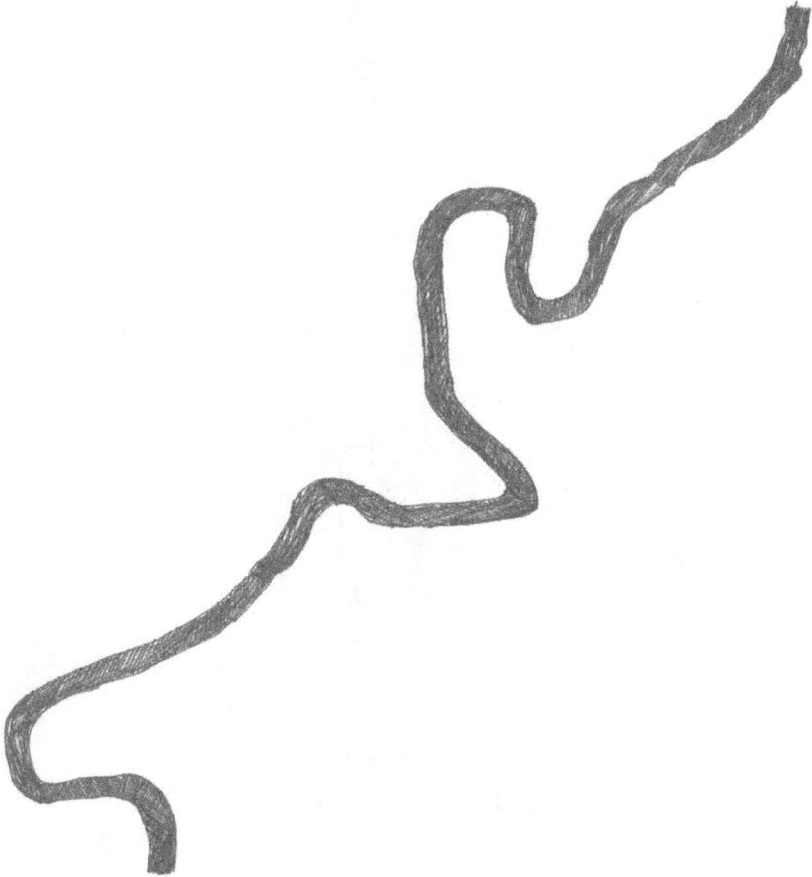

UNDERGROUND
RIVERS

By Justin Patrick Moore

Oneiric Imprint
Cincinnati, Ohio

SOTHIS MEDIAS

UNDERGROUND RIVERS
By Justin Patrick Moore
Oneiric Imprint, Sothis Medias
Copyright 2015 by Justin Patrick Moore.

ISBN-13: 978-0692395097
ISBN-10: 0692395091

The cover is an adaptation of Gustave Dore's *Charon* illustration from
Dante's *Inferno*.

THE KINGDOM OF HEAVEN
IN THE HEART OF THE CHILD

Strange voices of love
coodle in my ear,
beckoning me closer, drawing me
to the One I hold so dear.
Angels surround us,
    light as feathers
they guide my roving hands,
delivering me with a kiss
    into the promised land

into the sanctuary of her heart.
She is a Goddess
the full embodiment of bliss
with rose hued lips.
I blush and relinquish the grips
so that I may float in the night
to be held within her arms so tight,
where we may nuzzle under blankets of fuzz
with our bodies glowing
            and warm with the buzz of love.

Humming softly I sing to her my truest tune,
as it comes from the depths
                like a seed that has bloomed.
I offer her this gift of my voice
in a moment of ecstasy when all the stars rejoice
and all the Saints rain their blessings from above,
Heavens Kingdom descends swiftly as a dove.

We are licked by the soft caress of morning dew.
Halos encircle us.
We are embroidered into the fabric of God.
We are all children cradled in every fold
with helping spirits for our hands to hold.

In Memory Of:

My Mother,

Julie Anne Moore
May 31, 1952 - June 16, 2008

& my Grandmothers,

Mary Ann Moore
March 17, 1917 - July 28, 2012

Elissa Helena Cannon
September 25, 1933 - December 10, 2014

'With this the ghost of Lord Teiresias, its prophecy complete, drew back to the House of Hades. But I remained, undaunted, till my mother approached & drank the black blood. Then she knew me, & in sorrow spoke to me with winged words: "My son, how do you come, living, to the gloomy dark? It is difficult for those alive to find these realms, since there are great rivers & dreadful waters between us: not least Ocean that no man can cross except in a well-made ship. Do you only now come from Troy, after long wandering with your ship & crew? Have you not been to Ithaca yet, not seen your wife & home?"

-Homer, *The Odyssey*, Book XI

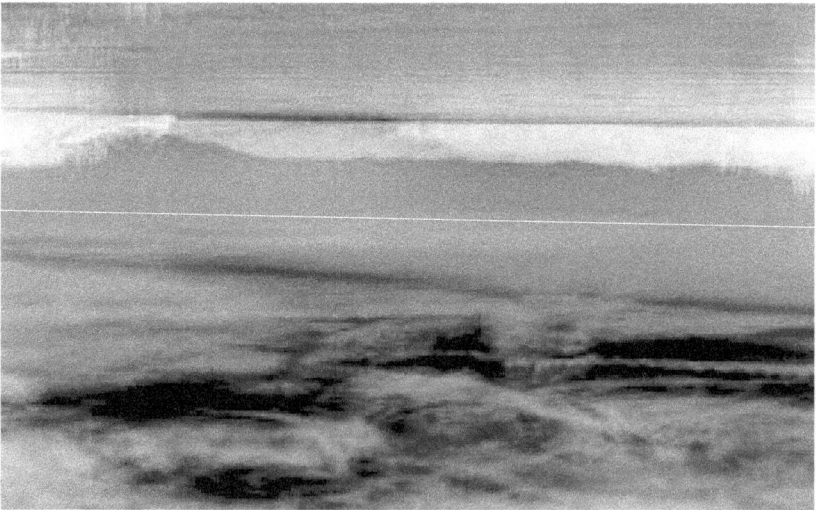

Acknowledgements

I would like to thank my Wife, the lovely Audriel, for her support. I am grateful for all she has given me: time for my years at the radio station, her encouragement and presence at talks and readings, sacrifices in helping me with plane fare when I needed to spread a message and stretch my abilities. Together we have walked in the woods and streets around the Miami Valley Watershed, the spiritual home of these poems. And listened to the creeks under the streets of our neighborhood after the rain.

Some of these works first appeared in the following publications: *For A Better World: Poems and Drawings for Peace and Justice* 2004, 2006, 2012, & 2015. *Silk Milk Magizain* spool #6. Various issues of *Silver Star: A Journal of New Magick*. The *Unprofessional* chapbook anthology of writers published by Aurore Press. The Spider first appeared in Oreyelle-Defenestrate Bascule's book *Time, Fate and Spider Magick* published by Avalonia. The October 2014 issue of *Aeqai* and the Autumn 2014 issue of *Cafe Review*.

CONTENTS

I. THE KINGDOM OF HEAVEN IN THE HEART OF THE
CHILD
II. WERID OLD AMERICA
III. BLIND AT THE TILL
IV. THE SPIDER
V. BLAZES IN THE BONE
VI. TAP ROOTS
VII. ROOTS CANAL
VIII. OKTOBERFEST, OHIO
IX. DREAMER OF THE DARK
X. MILL CREEK BLUES
XI. LEARNING TO SWIM
XII. THE COURTSHIP OF MA'AT
XII. FLY FISHING WITH SUN RA
XIII. UNDERWORLD GARAGE SALE
XIV. C IS FOR MURDER
XV. CAIN MARKS
XVI. GASAHOL
XVII. AFTER THE AFTER PARTY
XVIII. A SKETCH OF THEE HELLSCAPE
XIX. HOW TO BECOME A CONSPIRACY THEORIST
XX. THE CITY IS A DREAM
XXI. LUCIFERINS
XXII. PSYCHOACOUSTIC MEDICINE
XXIII. WHAT MAGIC IS
XXIV. THE ELECTRIC SNAKE BOOGY
XXV. FUNERAL FOR A PUNK ROCK JACKET
XXVI. THE RIVER STYX, REVISITED
XXVII. GOOSE SHIT RADIATOR
XXVIII. DIONYSIAN WINE
XXIX. THE HAND RETURNS TO IT'S WORK
XXX. UNDERGROUND RIVERS

WEIRD OLD AMERICA

There's an ole weirdo America
      my Granpa used to know
where horeshoes hung on painted signs
& hex's beamed from old barn doors.
It's hard to see now,
because the light from stores
clouds out stellar light
& the daily mind, trivial, has sunk low.

Too many bars
too much time
spent in them spent behind them

not enough
         down in cornfields
among the circled crops
of the Heart Land.

Down where the grass is blue
the moon used to shine
a midnight medicine when cold winds blow,
but now, with the steel factories closed
& the barn fallen over
with the trailer boarded up
all you hear are the ghostly echoes
      of that old weird America
the last plucked string
      of a homemade dobro.

Cause all the people have packed their bags
      to join the new Imperium,
called by the click & clink of coin
they've walked on & forgotten
the rusty drinking songs of coal barges,
      & neighborly waves & nods
local colors stripped like mountains

making way for Auto Malls.

Inside the big box walls,
John Henry's hammer can't be heard
       the railways been paved over
& their ain't no time for a strange birds call
the hoary haunts replaced by nowheres
a limbo of broken carts, emptied shopping lots.

pray the kudzu cover all

But there's a locket wrapped with hair
down deep in hidden pockets,
a heart pumping blood
among the oddballs & the lint,
amidst the shorn paper
      of the shorn people

within them:
untapped aquifers

subcutaneous reservoirs
where all secret rivers run.

BLIND AT THE TILL

The rutters have been ragged
though the sails on the mast are at full
the prow, set in its direction, to drift over the falls
as if the territory were just a map.
I don't know if it would be better or worse
to change directions, or maybe just relax:
my grip so tight on the wheel
the whites on my knuckles are showing.

I set out to claim a distant land
by the work of my own eye, with the sight of this hand
I've already left so many, so much behind
casting off from a dozen different ports
to a dozen dizzy cities, asking "what's my destiny?"

Now I'm afraid of mutiny if I again change course.

Only because I thought I was captain of this ship
& now come to learn I'm not even second mate
I thought the warp & weft were mine alone to weave
as if I could leave an offering of a few morsels at the sea
& steal the thread to stitch my own skein of fate.
I've given myself every chance to let this deceit sink in
& haven't questioned the orders I've received.

Now the winds of all my past are breathing full blast
the sirens of glamour lure me to their rocky scree.

The cunning whirlpool
                turns faster than the hand on my compass.
The inner flame
                is lanced about & ricocheted by hail.
The rocky reef protrudes its hungry teeth
as we head for the barren beach
to belly up & bottom out with the dying whales.

I could yet let my hand off the till
though water splashes & spills over the sides
I could let myself be pulled by the moon, by the stars
to be tugged along into strange & distant tides.

To let myself not know where it is I go
& stop trying to persuade the gods
to make clear the path I am to trod
but to go blind into the wine dark sea.

THE SPIDER

Spider, spider burning bright
in the luminous lunar light.
Fateful creature of earth & sky
spinning silk of space & time.

In what womb, moist & wet
were thy eight eyes placed & set?
How did you carry the fire
of words & web that so inspire?

& what poison that tips thy fang
can pause the life of what it stang?
Who to you so gave the power
to be the master of that hour?

What the silk? What the thread?
In what forge was your spirit bred?
What the pincers? What spreading glance
dares upon your weave to dance?

When heaven opens up its hall
& the pits of hell are revealed to all,
will you tremble upon your skein?
Or mark with ink your destined reign?

Spider, spider burning bright
in the luminous astral light.
Fateful creature of earth & sky
spinning silk of space & time.

BLAZES IN THE BONE

Some people say memories rise in the blood
to glisten in the rain when the muds been washed away,
the silt of years once over, once buried under stone
now burns in the marrow, now blazes in the bone.

The seasoned have learned
the elders know what's at stake
they've been kept awake by distant riddles
they have heard the harpers cry
the weird sigh of still more distant fiddles
the lung rattle as friends & lovers die.

These memories ache & will not be put away
they cannot be swallowed with hard or easy drink
they open on a pain that does not lead astray
a honed sword, they cut & cleave, bringing light into dark.

Pointing like darts into hallowed ground
where coffin wood roots grow deep
to the Tree that stands in the grove on a grave
where the Beloved Dead dream in sacred sleep.

Do not weep for me, the Willow says
for I am beyond your tears
live out your nights under Moon, under Stars
until your skin whorls from all the days of your years.

Some people say memories rise in the blood
to glisten in the rain, when the muds been washed away
the salt of life once over, once buried under stone
will burn once more in marrow, will blaze again in bone.

TAP ROOTS

To trace my ancestral tap roots, I sleep among bones
temple pressed against one stone pillow. To sing with the wind
I regress into the land, lathered in honeycomb, a cathedral of drones
swarm behind my eyes, unspooling thread, to mark how I descend.

I hear a rune, a psalm, whispered in the caverns dark
the ancient voice of a grizzly woman, awoke from hibernation
song lines flow from her spring, & the stars shoot sparks
as my fingers place the words into a glimmering constellation.

I climb down, scraping skin against bark, reaching for the boughs
slough it off. The garter snake suns itself on fossilized filigree.
The scorpion plants its poison to awake the crimson rose
& so ground me in the soil of my lawful pedigree.

To flourish, first decompose. Strip the pelt off the hart wood
sing the resuscitation of birds & change the course of the creek.
Nourish the headwaters of blind repose to become an ark in the flood.
Swim upstream, leap over hesitation's feet, wise as a salmon, & as sleek.

A DREAM OF THE GRAPHIC

ROOTS CANAL

The dentist is a boogeyman with an awl
whose X-Rays sink down into the bones
his drill bit gnashing the displaced stones,
tilling down teeth canal nerves until raw.

As winter thaws spring groundhogs give salute
& German farmers carve towpaths in the land
the work of shovels, mules, ropes & many hands
our history in dental records traced back to the root.

Now the Miami Valley is fractured from excavation
& the gaps in the mouth have received no implants,
the locks along the channel have slowly dissolved
to leave the fields beside the trench scrawny & scant
empty barns remain unfilled, feigned promises unresolved
from here to Eerie the landscape is a series of broken obligations.

St. Michael's Church & Cemetery, Fort Loramie, Ohio

OKTOBERFEST, OHIO

The cathedral of St. Michaels looms
as a megalith of staunch German stone
above the cornfields of Ohio's harvest.
Outside in the church yard, staunch German bones.

Up here in canal country everyone drinks
Budweiser in plastic half-liter steins
while the winds rip over the man-made lakes
vast but shallow. We dip potato cakes

in mustard on styrofoam plates. Huddled
under huge canvas tents smelling of sauerkraut
& unwashed liederhosen, laughing & dancing
with the oompah band, yelling at college football.

Someone adds wood to a fire, stirs ashes in the grate.
Beforehand the elders drank lager in the garage
& relayed memories. The montage of the past
slowly sinks into the soil, along with the grave markers

we visited on Oktoberfest morning. The way ahead
is a movie strip swiftly unreeling, a book of life
& a wheel of fate only sealed in part. The lips close
in silence the fishing line is cast with grains into the field.

Hell has been harrowed, death returns its yield.

DREAMER OF THE DARK

An ode in memory of Koizumi Yakumo:
Patrick Lafcadio Hearn

Lafcadio,
your Irish eyebrows
pour over paper
while your classic Greek hand
unfurls spindly writing
beneath diminutive lamplight.

Your one good eye is scrunched, myopic
your fingers cramped, back sore
head full of fantasy & folk lore,
the perfumed dreams of a fairy in a Tea garden.

You were a spiritual ambassador
for your final home in Japan,
adopted by the *Kami* as much by the people
from your birthplace on Lefkada,
by way of Dublin, Cincinnati
the West Indies & New Orleans.

Your gift was to tease out
the soul of a place,
to translate the *genius loci*
into a liquid language
soluble to friends
left behind in the West.

You were locked away as child,
shut in a closet, a punishment
to cure fears of the dark.
With age you end up going nearly blind,
befriending many ghosts along the way.

Your gift was inner sight.
In a playground game you lost an eye
but like Odin, became a seer
peering into Other worlds,
more at home in the Mittelmarch
then under the smoky towers of industry.
Your pen was made of foxfire
& all your words were goblin.

Washed up penniless in the Queen City
you slept on paper shavings
at the local printers,
nourishing your dreams in the library,
breathing in a host of fantastic heterodoxies.

Bootstrapped up from the pavement
you eventually landed behind a news desk.
Never afraid
you stared down the barrel of horror,
from violent cremations to tan yard murders;
immersing yourself in haunted landscapes,
listening for echoes, voices of ancient ancestors.

You did not mind bucking authority
even when it bucked you back.
Three glasses down, coming home from the beer garden
into the kitchen at the boarding house,
your eyes fell on Mattie, a black skinned storyteller.
The world wasn't ready for your illegal love,
cast upon the rocks of social disdain
you couldn't reach a safe harbor,
& your marriage, void under law, dissolved.

So you slinked on down to New Orleans
& simmered yourself in Creole cuisine,
hacking away at the papers again,
scribbling down many a fanciful sketch,
making attempts at translations from French,
growing your powers, pouring your light
into newsprint, denouncing corruption,
disabusing fallacy, penning obituaries
for Doctor John & Marie Laveau.

Then tiring of the Southern scene,
waxing weary of the socials while wanting the weird
you traveled even deeper south,
skipping off for two years to Martinique,
where you wooed the Muse of the odd
in search of tropical flavors
to quill your cryptic travelogues.

Then off again, pit stopping
in New York to wrangle with editors, publishers,
magazine men;
before tacking along on a train to Vancouver
to step aboard the good ship *Abyssinia*
on a Pacific passage dark as any of yours
& step off on St. Patrick's day in Japan 1890,
Yokohoma, among people who smiled,
wishing you well during the days torrential rain
dreaming at night of ideographs & insects
soundless visions running on phantom wheels.

In Matsue
you married during the frozen winter
Setsu the warm daughter of a Samurai,
who melted the coarser aspects of your nature.
There wasn't much language between you
so she spoke in the shared sympathy of Shinto
in the grave voice of her countries oldest chillers,

breathing life into ghosts,
awakening cruel demons who slept close to Earth.

Finding home at last you were made a citizen,
became professor Yakumo
gave birth to a son Kazuo
unleashed yourself on paper
letting the local spirits do the writing,
as your blood boiled under oil lamplight,
possessed, prolific, a passionate interpreter.

On good terms with *Kitsune*
the last years of your life were happy.

You made a boat of words
to crest over this rocky world of men,
& resting, sailed beyond them

your final voyage
off to visit the Hare in the moon
one last stop
on the river to Heaven.

Lafcadio Hearn

MILL CREEK BLUES

I.

Maketewa you were once called,
Maetewa once held in awe, you were
once a marshland
                  below the hillside forest
banks of cattails, otter families, dragonflies

sacred ground for those who made a home in this valley!

Alas Maketewa, what you once were
& what you have become
is no fault of the water itself.

As if you asked to staunch the flow
                of the little piglets blood
back in the day when
Spring Grove was a street of swine & mud
you stayed the course
even as the trickle of trichinosis
was sprayed downstream.

Now white ghost pigs fly
over the graves of the grove
as the trains squeal on by
past slaughterhouse remains
your shores still slick from the last flood.

Even your bloated carp
got sick off the hot dogs.

& it was all a Kahn anyway

Even the raccoons
wanted nothing to do
with the dumpsters
but washed their marbled hands
in your

malodorous brown soup of

lye & lime, black ink of
concentrated tanning liquors
hide trimmings, offal
glue, fertilizer, grease

where herons now wade in the shallow
workers wallowed, dumping the tallow

thinking you were just some serpentine ditch

who like the arms of a forgiving lover
continued to receive & remained open
even as the abuse compounded
your banks now home to impound lots
junk yards of reclaimed metal, car parts

the springs that dotted the valley capped with sewer lids

crows & vultures
circle diesel tracks

Mill Creek you were once called Maketewa!
Mill Creek you are now held at bay, arms length
even by those who just live a few blocks away.

We are not privy to your long suffering moods
as we no longer stand knee deep in your mud
in your water, we do not swim & play.
Maketewa you hold us in dismay
we who pissed in your pot
& left our chemical trails of dirty vapors
to mark where we settled, the way we came.

II.

     Alas!
The plastic bags tuck on sticks
choke hyperventilating frogs covered in black ick
now glow in Fernald fumes of marsh light
from everyday humdrum spills
as Proctor & Gamble empty their sink
as the MSD puts shit in our drink.

The creeks have been diverted to storm drains
the storm drains aimed at the Mill Creek
the bedrock converted to long channels of concrete
& fish don't swim but sink
from the bathwater bleach, from the poison
keep out of reach,
                children, keep out
poured down the sink
with all the crap from the hole that stinks

all creep into this divided basin
the east side from the west side
pigskin tiger pelts are our pride
       in this pork chop metropolis.

           False industry hides behind its tail.

Even the good ol' boys
       in the Mill Creek Yacht Club
          have a hard time setting sail.
Those boys gotta make sure
they got all their doctors shots

keep their immunity up.

Cause you ain't recovered
from your days as an open sewer
& you sure did stank it up.

III.

Underneath the bridge
sad old bums set up camp to sleep
next to sad twenty-something bums
who stay up all night, to keep warm
on burned shipping pallets
tomorrow, maybe, brings better luck
sign flying, hitching out his thumb
for someone to pluck a few singles from their wallet
& place into a worn out Starbucks cup.

       The forks in the road of fate seem as dry
       as Dry Fork Creek in high July
       & these fellas are just as thirsty
       enough to make a grown man cry.

Living broke off the Mill Creek is hard work
fishing for carp with nylon lines
all those bones to pick, like with Fred
who they had to kick out of camp
as he was fixin' to bring the popo down on their heads
what with his needles & all, & no thread
anyhoo, it ain't like americas got a shortage of tramps.

It's been a long time since the stream was full of trout.

But the down & out? We got that.
The wretched & tired, deep fried & true
we got them too. The poor from the harbor
the tempest-tost masses new to these shores
just up from West Virginia's door, last of the mountains
removed, yearning to breathe
free from the coal dust, but ain't no jobs
up here, no more, no more, no, no.

Floaters is what the coroners get
when persons unknown hit the road
& they get dragged up onto the ridge.
It's a pretty short bridge. So did they jump
into your thick cut loins lined with concrete slabs?

Prefab answers just won't do
when pulling jagged glass out of soles.
Children, you gotta wear your shoes!

& remember, don't drink the water.

LEARNING TO SWIM

It must be near half a mile
            across the Ohio river.
On the other side
            sycamores stripped of personality
only the white is showing
tangled around their roots
bleached driftwood from the creeks upstream.

From the public landing I launch
with only myself to fall back on now.
It gets deep quick, up to my waist
now my head goes fully under
& my feet don't reach the mud below.

Ancient carp stir from my thrashing
& I have to let go
            of the rucksack
containing all the family albums, photographs
& keepsakes acquired on the march.
All I can do now is drop it, paddle forth.

I'm careful not to let the water get past my lips
they are blue now, as are my feet, cold.
Last night's storm unmoored
                        another tree
        could I hitch a ride?

My heart races, I panic
looking at the distant shore

I must let go of the braided cord.

My hands become oars
to carry me across the wake
left by the Anderson ferry
but I find my clothes are weights

I once carried a loom
to play games with string
my fingers sang on the harp of yarn
& weaved new patterns
named after the stars.

Now my garments will be invisible
from the first hospital sheets
Mama wrapped me up in
to the three-piece suit I'll be buried in
all those vestments dissolve in the river

except the stitches over my heart pocket.

I don't see the bluegrass of Kentucky on the other side
but a desert whose sands are already in my eyes.

I cannot see the people at the landing anymore
but I do here a few voices call out to cheer me on
& I wave goodbye
my spirit brushing up to them in sleep.

Ahead of me

      the long trail to the luminous mountain.

THE COURTSHIP OF MA'AT

Justice is the sword of an angel
   prodding your heart open
& stuffing it with peacock feathers;
Justice is a vulture in the desert
 who chews your flesh to expose the bone.

She is the fear you feel at the threat of death
    when a change of heart
     might just be a shift on the scales.

Where do you sit in the balance?

One false breath might trigger an avalanche.

Justice will blanch you in the pan
  & cut you open to smell your blood
  taste what you are made of.
After all, she is used to roadside pickings.
She is blind & looks straight into you

another corpse on her chopping block.
      Will you step up?

Do you fear a harsh mistress?
Then master the tasks given to you
& prepare your shoulders for more.
The road up the mountain gets steeper yet.

She's not the kind of girl
who you can just hand a wish list to.

If you piss her off
she might just throw you to the crocodiles.

Her throne does not exist for your whim.
The playthings of her wiles come home burned.

She doesn't pity little grown boys playing soldier
or those who weep in the night.
She teases out the secrets you've kept wound tight
& exposes them, sober, on a cold days light.

The path to the court of Ma'at is one of dread & joy.
If you seek her home along the banks of the Nile
bring the gift of your empty hand, or prepare to be spurned
she won't be bribed.

She'll churn your guts inside out, settle your debts, scatter your doubts.

Walk with her as she cleans up the recent dead
staying level, decent, severing life's threads
preparing your own bed for the last breath
when her father is weighed against your heart.

FLY FISHING WITH SUN RA

I went fly fishing with Sun Ra last night.

We waded into particle fields of ice
to sit on the edge of Saturn's glistening ring
& drink the venom of the Desert
while we talked about gravity

music is what really holds the world together
he says, pointing his finger, an electric conductor

of the spheres in their orbit, of the satellites spinning
the old band leader grinned as we cast our lines

Sun Ra's bait danced on the surface of the cosmos
his fingers were fly, on the black & white keys
shifting harmonic perspectives, rippling in the drift
a whippoorwill of melody, his piano a vortex

our civilization is like Atlantis, ya dig
caught in histories undertow, human larvae
only just now awaking, percussive rhythms shaking
off the sorrow, awaiting a great tomorrow.

Ra tells me about his time as an ambassador
of Fibonacci thought forms, of his work
on asymmetrical equations & alien syntax,
as a musical guide, to the stars in the underworld

> all he has to do is flash his badge
> to Anubis at the security checkpoint
> & we pass between the pylons
> guarding the moon

& so angle in the stream of stars
as we carry baskets woven from cattails
traveling down strange celestial roads
to the sound of a sistrum, as the cymbals shift
& vectors change, we lift off to an *other* plane

we haul in our last catch

always leaving enough spawn to regenerate the Nile
so decide to catch a rocket skipper,
stow away our gear & go trawling

across the arched body
of the heliocentric worlds.

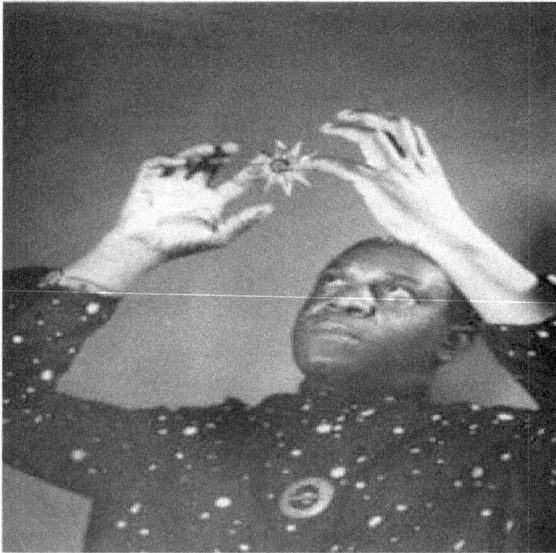

UNDERWORLD GARAGE SALE
(Parallel Universe Version, Take 2)

I.
Come Saturday morning I get a ring from Uncle Dan
  the other end of the phone somewhere in limbo,
asking me if I want to join him
     out on the garbage picking rounds

round & around we go
over the rivers & through the snow.
He knows what parts of me are still missing
how torn apart I am, a part of me here
a part of me there, locked in my apartment.
He hands me the Marlboros from the glove compartment.
He knows how I lost my head
      over heels
      over the bridge

Is that it floating down the River Styx, Ohio?

Uncle Dan commands the wheel, a veteran
chauffeur of snakes still fighting with the Viet Cong.
His internal arguments last all night, as does his laughter
his chatter, so we tune the mental radio to a new song
preferring the moments between station & station,
ears digging into splattering static, eyes trained on the curb
junk hunting in bins, dig in, dig in
despite the bags in the attic
    already being full of marbles & mice.

I am saturated by the schizophrenic atmosphere of Dan's Dodge

      smoke rings
      donut holes
      gasoline vapor

We circulate the streets scanning the scatter
snagging boxes of cassette tapes & 45 platters
            a slowed down loop, disintegrating
as aging jocky clubbers now in rockers
clean out there long term storage.

We head down to Cleve's & comb the banks of the Great Miami
            she coughs up more than driftwood & rubber tires
sometimes scrap metal, & buffalo pennies left for the ferryman.

We head back up to Delhi from River Road
I take note of auspicious signs:
crows flying north, turkey vultures circling the rail yard

& GARAGE SALE
Corner of West 8th St. & Enright

-Just next to St. Joe's cemetery right?

Dan tells the story of going AWOL from the marines
stealing a cab & taking strange snakes for rides
arrested, discharged, locked up in a mental ward

don't tread on me.

II.

The place is fairly sinking into the soil of Price Hill
the garages old fiberglass doors on jangled tracks
brown window panes, the grinning teeth of Behemoth
with smells of old sweet & sour lawnmowers
rotting grass, nectarines.

A black rat serpent slides down from the rafters
& slinks into the hedge. Dan freezes
-another one of my customers, he says.

There are nine round tables in this pit
so we circle them, looking for the relics of forgotten saints.

This is an old man's puttering chateau
a monument of lost hope
a zone of utter coldness, mud & diarrhea
of forgetting & remembering
                                    the dismemberment
a place to brood
hovering over broken consumer electronics

of wood, wool & cottage cheese
where ancient shoe polish still shines the soul.

III.

On the first table:
an anthology of local poetry

on the second table:
stacks of Playboy magazines
photos of girls on trampolines

on the third table:
gravy boats & cotton bibs
wind chimes made from barbecued ribs

on the fourth table:
money clips & poker chips
outdated books on stock market tips
& an empty wallet

on the fifth table:
a smashed cordless phone
a picture of heads buried in sand
tapes of metal, & CDs
all music of fury, elastic hair bands

on the sixth table:
tarot cards, marijuana
a black crystal ball, a pentacle
a paperback copy of the gnostic gospels
all laid out on the apron of a Freemason
on the seventh table:
G.I. Joe army,
shotgun, pistols, bayonets
knives, brass knuckles
& a submachine gun

on the eighth table:
a self portrait in oil
a movie stars memoir
the diary of a con artist
self help books (how to hustle)
a pimps cane, a bankers ledger
leaked documents from congress
yellow papers served from a lawyer

on the ninth table:
a sword, a plowshare
Cain's rotting cornucopia
the dried skin of an adder
a framed picture of Robert Johnson
ice skates for the frozen lake
thirty pieces of silver
a plate empty
but for one pair of dentures.

We then emerged to see again the stars.

C IS FOR MURDER

A melodramatic corpse
sooths the mind
this corpse, a corpse like no other,
exquisite victim of pathos, full of juxtaposition

a soothing criminal
in a manner, is a mastermind
a maker of melancholy
a villain whose machinations
make for a quiet evening of murder.

A fit subject for any setting:
an Italian villa
an English vicarage
a mist shrouded Scottish village, fishermen
a Southwest ranch, cowboys
a harbor harboring, sailors, stolen goods
a slipknot ripe for murder.

For the sum of lots of money
a heroine on heroin
poisons an ailing heiress
securing the family fortune
secreted in an offshore account
takes on a new identity

or perhaps a kidnapping
only the ransom was paid
destruction waylaid
but wait, the blood was already
on the frayed cuffs of his jeans

splatter from the first cut:

a different victim

grass on the gym shoe
the certain texture of a bootprint
pubic curlicues, spittle, torn cloth
wayward clues in a forensic universe

or was the victim simply brained
by falling masonry?
gray matter jettisoned from the body
like hijacked cargo from the orient express

or did he die of innocent lockjaw?
from botulism or fear of talking?
lest someone take out a hit
"don't ever, ever let anyone else know
what you saw bobbing in the pay lake
on your weekend fishing trip"
the mob boss goonie says

a small dose of toxicology should do the trick
letters glued under fingernails, ears found in fields

curved pipe in hand
a fine job for any weekend sleuth.

CAIN MARKS

For those of us marked by Cain
there may be no outward sign
just an awakening of the blood
a tingling of the brain
as once silent voices whisper memories
of the violent choices made by the founder of our line.

For such whose eyes have been swaddled
for those who now dwell in the dark
from the recesses of an ancient cave
comes the shower of anvil sparks!

The hammer cries out resplendent
on the steel forged in fire & ice
the swords sting is unrepentant
till turned into a plowshare to furrow fields
as the first farmers sow the grain of life.

For such as you who are bread makers
or know the ways of the horse
stirrers of the cauldron & keepers of the hearth
who despise the wealth of tyrant kings
& their minions who tear down woods
be firm in your knowledge, in your second sight
even as you become soil, food for the growing worms.

You have known toil & trouble
watching as boughs break, as hunters make spoil
only to find yourself in the kitchen, dough in your hand
wandering when the soldiers will depart the Land
& leave these Seven Hills in peace.
Or will they continue to plunder until all is asunder,
until the fields are barren with grief?

This is the mark of care on our shoulder
the burden & exaltation we take from life to life
we sow plants in the garden under new moonlight;
as cast outs from Eden we saved seeds from the first
a song of serpents is on our tongue, as cloven as our feet.

Ours is the gnosis transmitted in dream
from the origin of fire to this waning age of steam,
marked out, the Flaming Sword setting us aside
we Zig-Zag back & forth on our lightning trail to the Grail,
in shadows we grow & in shadows we stride!

GASAHOL

The oil in my mouth
tastes like lies
all the chemical untruths
are slick petroleum
on my tongue that slide

I want to spit it out
but the distillates are between my teeth
gumming up the works
a smoldering fire water,
that chokes me as I breathe

my lip linings are saturated
the wound sutured, washed with gasoline
a sick alcohol poison
that bites with a venomous sting

& my words
are the fossil fuel fumes
burning up dangerous emotions
sending them off into the atmosphere
of fear
tetraflurocarbons
invisible monoxide gas
released in daily portions
sitting at the bar, I have another glass.

AFTER THE AFTER PARTY

After
        the after party
America woke up
with a hangover
After
        all the oil was guzzled
doing keg stands
        at wells around the world
guns held
to the face of foreign frat boys.

We were raiding

tipping the scales in our favor
when free trading broke
because the spoils were in other lands

we'd blown up our own mountains
poisoned our own shores
crude treated coats on one thousand seals
& bloody sputum in our lungs

the black coal dust on our hands
didn't stop us from signing off those deals

After
        the after party
we woke up shaky
because the pipes were cashed out
the last glimmer of ancient sunlight
burned in a frenetic
threehundredyearorso flash

woundtight to our gadgets
the screens glitching out
into digital cold cloud

war fever
post traumatic vets sent home
when the last barrel sold

in desperation for more
a club soda golf swing
offshore
desecrating gulf coast

& we wonder, still wasted
after
        all the fun has been had
who's going to clean up after us,
after the after party?

Isn't that a third world job?

learning, as the fuel burns out
we just might need to use our own hands

A SKETCH OF THEE HELLSCAPE

In the trenches I have dreams
   of bell-drops falling from a neutron sky.
Wicked planes of deceit are hovering
above broken cities of ash,
where children lay strayed out.

Across the horizon, fading into a grim dusk
   white flashes race away distantly
   searing the air with nuclear visions.

I hear the myriad screams
          blistered memories
burnt with boiling holy water onto my brain.
They succumb unto relentless sickness.
Shadows etched onto concrete graves.

From the trenches I feel the sweat drops sting
          shrapnel of war all around me flies
buzzing on festering carcasses, tainting the water
   feverous hellscapes swarm in malaria skies.

HOW TO BECOME A CONSPIRACY THEORIST

First, go to the library & check out 23 books
on 23 different subjects.
Make sure a few of them are about political intrigue,
a couple about the mafia, & a few about the Roman Catholic Church.
Still others are going to be about Nikola Tesla, Wilhelm Reich
or other neglected renegades of science.
Don't forget the tomes about undercover aliens, the Roswell cover-up,
& the secret Grail bloodline of the Knights Templar.
& it wouldn't be an exemplar theory of conspiracy
if you didn't have at least one pedophile priest on the lam as a
Freemason.
So much for the basic list of ingredients.
If you're really determined to become a conspiracy theorist,
(it takes balls of sweaty steel, & more than a quarter ounce bag of
determination)
then you're going to have to find a way to get yourself abducted,
have a chip implanted in your head, or better yet, your prostate.
That's where they stick the butt plug probe after all.
You'll know you are being gang stalked when your ass starts to jiggle &
twitch.
You absolutely cannot be a conspiracy theorist
without at least one, preferably two dozen minus one,
obsessive compulsive delusions.
Something that will drive you to research declassified documents
files where all the names have been blacked out,
a need as strong as the CIA-Mobs when they drove a bullet into JFK
(it's not a conspiracy theory unless he is mentioned at least three times).
Assassinations galore, & hostile Central (intelligence) American
takeovers
covert operations where Hitler's inglorious clones hit the street in drag,
will form the bedrock of your paranoid speculation.
These are the bread & butter of any bona fide conspiracy, make no
mistake
because the government has a stake in making sure your book never
sees print.

That's why your chronicles of the time-traveling misadventures
of Elvis & Jimmy Hoffa, including the time they pulled the butt plug
on JFK,
making sure to wipe him off their bucket list & the face of the Earth,
have to be published on an obscure blog
with images you got from the random button on 4chan.
But you can't write using your own computer, not that you have one.
So you hang out in the tech center at the library hoping to leave no
trace.
Either way you get the feeling the Feds are shoulder surfing,
locking on to you, their main target & threat, for the dastardly deeds
you uncovered.
They've got keystroke recognition, & your apartment is under 24/7
surveillance.
You're starting to think the evil landlord is taking a cut,
reporting your every move.
It's unfortunate but now might be the time
to dump the underage girlfriend. You are sure she is a snitch.
Besides, you didn't like the results she got on her last pregnancy test.
Leaving the library you go to the diner with a box full of scribbled
notes,
hoping you might get a chance to meet Agent X.
No dice. He doesn't show up, so over two pots of coffee
you ask yourself what JFK would have done in such a situation.
That's when you have the penultimate realization
that you don't have Marilyn Monroe's phone number anyway
& your cell phones been hacked.
After the first cup from the third pot
your rectum starts to twitch. As you squeeze your sphincter
you know the man across the room is tracking your every move.
It's a GPS thing. They can make you
take a crap on yourself, anywhere, anytime. A ticking fecal time bomb.
Because you're wired in. One push on the button
& your electrode starts to ditch whatever is in your bowels.
You squeeze again & hope they don't push that button,
so you do your best to surreptitiously ignore
the man in black ordering cherry pie to go.
The waitress Claire really wants you to go.
You've taken up a four top all through the lunch rush
& you only ate a bagel.

But if you want to be a conspiracy theorist
it's a no-no to ever leave a decent tip.
Fuck man, don't the corporations owe you enough?
Just focus on cutting up miscellaneous passages from your notes.
Shuffle them around in your Rastafarian hat.
For a honkey with dreadlocks it doesn't look bad on you.
Claire must be on the "inside".
Why else would she be glaring at you like that?
Or maybe she has the hots for you & wants to take you home, get into
your pants.
Reassembling the text you have found impossible connections.
& now that your spider senses are tingling
you know it won't be long before the reptilians unveil themselves
with their decrepit hunger for fermented milk & domestic cats.
They are at the top of the Pyramid of Power.
No, your brains are not old & scrambled.
Yes, you would like another refill.
You've still got an hour to kill
before you can catch the bus to Joe's to score some more weed.

THE CITY IS A DREAM

Faces both familiar & strange,
curve through the mystic canopy
of skyline skylights.
Grey men move into mercantile ziggurats
    holding hostage time,
sit in plush rooms, smoke cigars,
above the People's marketplace
(a quaint breeding ground
    for redneck carnivals,
a pulpit for clownish impresarios).

The City is a Dream
    of a full moon, a blood moon
    an invitation to a scarlet masquerade,
written on an old postcard
whose memory is never the same.

The City is yearning, desirous
exultant in the reckless passions
executed by youths,
        (eased into
with wrinkled hands holding old age)
    behind one hundred doors
    soaked into the love stained sheets
of a thousand boudoirs,
a condom thrown from the shotgunned window
    of a pimped out gangsta car.

The City is a Nightmare factory
    of dripping chemicals bleaching ancient shells,
      a bricked over canal covering ancient hells,
an underworld of secret pipes & drains,
graffitoed in the calligraphy of fire:
      hash smoking sultans
    hide harems in the sewers.

Paved over, the street tops are pock marked
like the faces of snout nosed politicians
            who ride across in motorcades
their tongues crooked,
                forged from broken blades.

The City is a Palimpsest
        a lingering note on a musical score,
long forgotten, locked in a dusty drawer.

The City is a Cemetery
whose dead aren't laid to rest
(children step off yellow school buses
                into puddles splashing rain
not singing the cemetery song)
only the dirge is heard, struck at cathedrals
            on clockwork hours, marking the beginnings
            of endless rotework shifts,
sleepwalking, the grey men dead suits
            drift into

dreams of invisible cities
where friendly dogs lick the coal ash
        off the face of a chimney sweep.
Dreaming of internet cities
                constructed from blinking lights
red lights inside the crackhouse parlors
where vapor trails of crystal smoke
            vivisect the night;
            consumed by sordid dreams
inside bickering brothels
            of carnal pleasures & venereal spite,
where the puttanesca is as cold
            as the John left to breathe
            his last asphyxiated dream.

The City is a parking lot
    built over your grandpas baseball field,
a meadow of screeching whales
     as trains bleed into the harbor.
Incest knows the city
    as does dishonor & Victorian disgrace
the City is a kingdom of illegitimate sons,
                     fallen princes,
a place where birds fashion nests
from old braided nylon weaves & fast food wrappers,
where sleeping bags are unfurled beneath the overpass.

The City is a jaundiced liver
              fortified by wine,
a fecund blister, a conundrum
sticky as the bubblegum on the bottom of a shoe.

The amusement park is a City
    waiting to be dumpster dived,
a menu whose restaurant is never the same
a library of Babel whose voluptuous pages
electrify the fatigue of a fog smoked brain.

The City is a ruse,
    a weary mirage enticing neon travelers.
The City is a sphinx
    of many headed riddles,
a phantom trajectory
    whose presence cannot be traced.

LUCIFERINS

I was born into a culture
        of nebulous phosphenes.
My eyes, from rubbing,
had built in floaters
                specks of luminosity
electric sparks charging the visual battery.

I threw a rock into a purple lake

(memory recall recalls memories
distant faces distant past)

deep below the ground
clunking through a fissure
startling a jelly fish, it hung
perched with clenched tentacles.

It slinked & I followed
underneath black ice waves
past cave white crays
& blind shrimp

I wanted to reach bottom
touch the cracked stalactites
but my lungs ached
shivering from the undertow
ecstatic cold,
& dreams of oblivion

screaming empty bubbles,
my bronchia filled with brine
then I saw the Kraken
sitting on a nest of jewels,
his glowing Luciferins shined.

PSYCHOACOUSTIC MEDICINE

Controlled bleeding
                        is my preferred method of doctoring
as a chance to cut is a chance to cure.
It's time for a facelift
as long as it ain't no plastic surgery disaster.

In this theater of memory
the only operations not on display
are the cleaning of my tools on the autoclave
after the skin was resewn
from where it was torn at the fray.

I've been listening to soundtracks
whose movies are yet unmade,
& I've been searching for suture
in sonic landscapes
trying to escape the auto da fe
to ease on down this road, still unpaved.

The hardest thing has been restringing the banjo
the harp of New Albion
because when I crane my neck to listen, it strains
all I hear are tortoise shell echoes,
lost in the din of the city.

We are so close to the landing strip
all I ever hear is music for airports
never the fashion or the fame of the runway.
That's why I've had so much trouble
following my own trains
faraway thoughts are passing by

leaving me breathless.

I knew I'd need to spend more time
breathing but its winter
below freezing is hard on the lungs,
& on the microscopic lifeforms in the soil;
I'm waiting to be wheeled in a new air supply
it'd be my dirt of luck if it was helium, or nitrous oxide
to make the stars of my lid spin.

Only just now I feel like a deerhoof
hit me in the kidney, & I'm burning
so fast it scares me, in my coffin
I've been making maps & atlases
of the Underworld, so ready for the sun to hit.
I cry out to the universal mother
for the faith & courage
to reach for a new order,

to listen to the stethoscope on my heart.

I call on the Elf power of the smoke Fairies.
& seek Elf protection as I search for the hidden stone.

If the ambulance died in the poets arms
then a new Balance must be attained.

Heaven's blade is double edged after all.

Can I inch towards the gates of dawn
without going mad?
The crazy diamond will shine on
& music will always be a part of my medicine, man

Father Asclepius incubated me
to suffer a sickness of snakes
now they writhe, ready to escape

The channels on my psychic TV
are showing strange fascinations
snow static, a person I can't trace

so turn off my mind
just drifting.

It's a dark age of love these days,
for those who swim in a cathedral of flames
down lost rivers, into secret domains

WHAT MAGIC IS

Magic burns somewhere
between phosphorous & philosophy
it churns the midnight soil
after hopping the cemetery wall.

"Dig this," it says
pointing to an unmarked grave.
Magic wasn't made
to be an energy slave
whim of yours to hire
black lace & red light
for the convenience of your desire.

Sometimes it is a thirst
slaked by snagging you into the coals
a wild mare giving birth to foals
the snare is, its out of your control.

Who lights this match now smells the sulfur
it doesn't demand you be pure
but is a catalytic converter of events.

Sometimes it is better not to know.

What is it I am doing? What is it all for?

The horizon is a door.

THE ELECTRIC SNAKE BOOGY

The Fakir had cultivated the venom of his winged cobra with such care and erudition that connoisseurs of the ecstatic delights gained from poison came from all corners of the kingdom to sample its bite. As is frequently the case among addicts there were those who overestimated their resilience to tolerate the effects of the reptilian substance. Feeling the pinch of the Uraeus at the base of the spine and subsequent flooding of the sensorium with inexplicable tinglings, sensing the emanations of the stars, was known, in some, to cause madness & death.

So the Fakir Srikanth was never surprised when his assistant Legrange, a dirty French emigre, had to drag another casualty down to the bone yards alongside the river. The first time a corpse came back, blackened but not burned, revivified, breathing, intact, it did surprise him. It was a strong venom indeed which took a man so deep into a coma as to resembled death. Of these cases, & there were only a few, the celebrant of the serpentine mysteries often reported such vivid encounters in the supernal realms as to defy even the the Fakir's ratiocination. With supreme dread & fear he reluctantly sent the poisoned back out into the world. They had been torn apart & were in need of healing. Yet he was no healer. His hand was not for mending. They walked away from his shack, back into the desert, wounds gaping wide.

He rued that word from these few fortunate unfortunates would somehow spread, & the respect he had earned for genetically engineering such fine specimens as the winged snake would be ruined. Only the opposite was true, & those who had been so close to becoming ash came back to test once again their temper & strength against the fire of the serpents venom. & they brought with them devotees eager to submit themselves to the hand of chance, people fervent to partake of the miracle themselves. So it was that many pilgrims began slithering to the Fakir's once humble dwelling. & so his pride began to swell as did his purse with gifts received from the many petitioners desirous of the ineffable poison. Indeed, his now frequent visits to the brothel, his commanding swagger & sway among the people of the nearby village who feared his art, all combined to attract the attentions of the Heresiarch.

The electric chair of the inquisitors had been sitting dry for many a year as the populace had finally succumbed to his lashings. Yet the Heresiarch was eager for the high he got when he made another man taste the juice. There was nothing quite like watching eyeballs boil to a blister in the socket. When he want to the Fakir's dwelling he hadn't counted on being taken in by the strange rhythms of the circle of snake charmers whose somnolent pipings now attended the increasingly elaborate services of the Fakir.

Soon he was among them, the sweating poor and merchants alike, among the warriors & converted priests, among the flying reptiles amidst the celebrants. All burned with violent inebriation. The snakes were hungry & ready to pounce.

FUNERAL FOR A PUNK ROCK JACKET

The punk rock jacket I wore
to announce my colors

was old, army green
 sweat sleeves stained

frayed edges fastened
with disposable bic lighter clips
patches half stitched
to flap in the wind
others safety pinned

with plenty of buttons
to flaunt favorite bands.

Hanging in my closet
unworn for over thirteen years
it was a cloak
holding old resentments & angers in harbor:

> *rage against the machine issues*
> *a writ of agitprop opposing the teenage matrix*
> *I wanted to huff the fumes*
> *of an Atari teenage riot*
> *an adrenalin shoot out, nerves on the fry*

The smell of those years has long been rancid.

My morning jacket was a sheet
over German Catholic night convulsions
with its black, red, & yellow flag,
runes scrawled in a protective hex
in sharpie pen & marker on the convex
all dolled up, wearing a mask of Gothic masquera
& the eyeshadows of insomnia
& the halo of a chimera.

It was my blanket
to hunker down in scratches of honeysuckle
on the end of a suburban Blue Ash street
where we half-slept for the night after the festival
as hallucinatory sirens & helicopters dithered
the phantom cops hovered in twilight, surrounded
telling us to stick up our empty hands.
It sat with me on a moldy couch on Elm street,
some convenient tenant had thrown to the curb,
in front of the cigarette store at the bus stop
so we plopped down to broken springs
all the stuffing coming out as I unraveled
hoping I hadn't missed the last 21 back to Westwood.

> *An old gentleman drunk fell to his knee*
> *took our picture & staggered back into the*
> *midnight streets.*

Vampira my pet rat crawled in the armpit
of my punk rock jacket, she huddled in the cleft.
Together we smelled of French fries & patchouli
& downtown brown dirtbag weed
Solomon the wise ass Rastafarian swindled to us
after buying us underage forties
we had to drink with him in the alley next to Corryville Kroger.
My jacket moshed in the racket
of Dixie trashed chicks puking on the stoop
& hung over with the downwardly mobile home
trailer park citizens of Florence, Kentucky Y'all.

I threw the old thing out just this week.
Its entire arcana of anger
a bled out canker
is to be buried without ceremony
married to earth, compacted at Rumpke
into the mountain of trash, its final resting place.
I've got other hides to wear
the thick pelt of a bear.

This new skin is of tooth & claw
of berries & salmon in a slobbering jaw.
This new skin is a storm on the land
a berserk warrior with a sword in his hand
in a fleece of polar fur
to wrap close as I tunnel underground
into standing stones, barrows & mounds.

THE RIVER STYX REVISITED

I.

Under the black cherry, as February
wind sweeps against the furred & feathered
friends the scent of laurel & pine throb

are a drum in the blood.

                    Wilderness approaches

this is the only classroom,

out on the land, surrounded by burial mounds.
The sky is the color of soot, below the garden
is sleeping, limp roots in frozen ground.
Lopped off grape vines yet to crawl back
onto the rusted fence planted in dark earth.

A mountain looms ahead in the gloam
whose switchback travels of gravel & salt
dissolve into the powdered snowcap of the sun.

The brimming cup of death promises this ascent.

For now there is buttered bread in the morning,
but sooner or later the river is opened up
her two banks the covers of a worn out prayer book
our dark appointments scribbled in the margins

do not resuscitate but breathe out
the last labored whispers recite the text.

& bring a coin to the crossing for safe passage
& bid farewell to the swollen moon, trees
& sun on your cheek
as the body falls away.

II.

One by one by one, her friends all fell.
their entrances & departures
all mapped out, marked as crossroads
remembered with a stone.   Grandmother points at the crows.

Out one door & into another one,
the revolving whirlpool of stars
the evolving vortex
of one life after life after life.

Whether burned half fast & so bright
or churned slow in the mill
all fall down, dead leaves ruffling
the bodies building emptied, the tenants moved out
into strange landscapes
one after one, passing & pausing in indifferent space.
Did the world begin with the call of a crow?
Does the hand that harrows the land reap what is sown?
One hard lesson after another
or a harvest?
either/or
delivered without fanfare
either/or
carried without delay

so many cries echo on the mountain.

While people on this side of the river still shake
just as trees do in February wind
great feats of eye & hand & of magic fade

throughout all this round turning of the world
& knowledge gained still muddied by the seasons
over the odd & even over the years, is life tangled.

Grandmother is still
counting crows
her fingers yet knitting a new caul.

GOOSE SHIT RADIATOR

Years ago I walked the daily dog
at Salway park, between the Maketewa
a.k.a the Mill Creek, & Spring Grove Cemetery
& watched as the Great Dane galloped
     as massive cotton wood tree tops swayed,
to mingle with obelisks, to pierce the ragged skyline.
It was late summer, just before Harvest Home
festival season almost over, & I was careful
to step over the sink hole of what had passed.
The cold wind was coming in, so I lifted my tongue
in praise to the North whose gusts traveled
over Great Lakes & amber rust belt plains
to clear the smog of the Cincinnati air
all the way down from the Arctic circle, by way of Canada.
Geese droppings littered the soccer field
my big Blue Merle looked for her own place to crap
& I thought of the green algae pools in the graveyard
of the fossils in the bedrock lining the creek
& all the suburban lakes from Westchester to Batavia
how the birds recline & dip in these shallow lakes
   refusing to migrate.

Out on Stonelick Road at the tail end of the dog days
  we took our grandson to feed the ducks
day old gluten free buns, & crusts of rye
leftover from the Labor day grill out.
We walked around the pond, stagnant heat
of the gated condo community
refuge for retirees afraid of being accosted
by Jehovah Witnesses waiving copies of the Watchtower.
Thunder rolled in & the sky outside turned frightful
   inside the TV spins delightful colors,
a technicolor coat against the gray.

Mesmer would have been proud of my lost generation.

Watching the weather channel, away from the clouds
  a wall screen window safe from the freak hail.
The four year old is playing video games
old mother goose replaced by a palm pilot
instead of making shapes in the lightning torn cumulus.

We deserve to be attacked by the angry birds
who swoop in front of our cars, swarming or singular.
Reminds me of the time my Dad had to pull one out of the grill
on our way to Chatanooga. It got my attention.
Murderous crows now return from rural roosts
back to winter in the city for the dark half of the year
after the veils thinned, we remain.
Underneath their black visage, beaks pecked at garbage
white fast food bags torn open in the dumpster
behind Clifton Natural Foods.
I now hold the feathered end of a rattle
to shake & to storm & to call down the geese.
Colonel Sanders appears to me in vision
burning in the deep fryer of his own grease
a wishbone lodged in his throat.
Chickens flock to his old Kentucky home
to peck at the fingers he licked from the bone
a chorus of morning bird calls now muffle his shrieks
all in a ruffle, I lead him down the cavernous deep
crowned as a dunce with his buckethead
only his sagging sack of skin remains
so I leave him for dead, a meal for the roadside vultures
Someone must carry on, decomposing culture,
  & carry on with the carrion

-& the baggage, you ask?

Leave it behind.

DIONYSIAN WINE

Drinking the wine of the Silver Dusk
inhaling the red inked hue
imbuing burgundy visions
sipping distillations of the pineal dew

we have all gathered
behind the scarlet drapes
to take our places on the checkered floor
we hold the golden key
that unlocks the silver door
into twilight
betwixt the sun & moonnight
enacting rituals of change
-constant as the seasons
clothed in shadow, dancing strange shapes
threshing wild grapes,

                    the harvest is in

purple stains on our souls feet

THE HAND RETURNS TO ITS WORK

I do not want to sever my hand,
throw the hacksaw at the other,
& leave the job unfinished.

I must find a way to staunch this land,
rejoin the tissue of finger trees
& the rivers arteries.

How could I assault myself in this way,
by taking an axe to that which lets me breathe?
It must be my left hand setting down a Dionysian path
thinking he has old Apollo cloaked & deceived.
Rightly so, the right hand wishes to chop
the left hand which learns the Craft by intuition,
the right, by sealing up the drafts,
appraises workmanship.

Application remains the only way to get the paint down
& steady rhythms can drum up water from the deep.
There is an old rock in the crook of the stream
furrowed by time, stone it remains
inseparable, one is the bed the other splashes over.

Given enough practice anyone can make wine,
but the vintner is most at home
culling from the vines of old generations, brought over
to New Albion, the joy of one cups trickle
imparted by ancient oak.

 & with smoke
once again clouding the head
the hand returns to its work.

UNDERGROUND RIVERS

Underground rivers
      run in rivulets

sunken streams branch
into thousand veined tributaries
beneath the earth's skin,
trickling over smooth stones
to swirl in ancient vortices
spiral into deep caverns
& bubble up in sacred wells.

I've traced you over cobblestone.
I've listened to your echoes
at the sewer grate after the storm
& wandered deep in your pipes
swimming pale as a blind worm.

I've paced alongside you
on trails seldom walked, overgrown with weeds,
& watched your waters drift into culvert & canal.

Since you've been drained into countless diversions
my only wish has been to break up
the callous concrete beds you've been laid in,
underneath streets & dry creeks;
my fierce dream has been to drink from your cup
saturate the dry barren clumps
of parched rock & ground thirsty for relief.
Your course may have strayed,
forced as a fugitive from your first bed
driven into asylum by expansion & industry

  yet never disappearing
& when the first hurricane rain drops
appear from the south after heavy drought
your secret sluice is sought.

On the day when you rise
from deep beneath the ground
I will be there to meet you
 at the wrought iron gate.

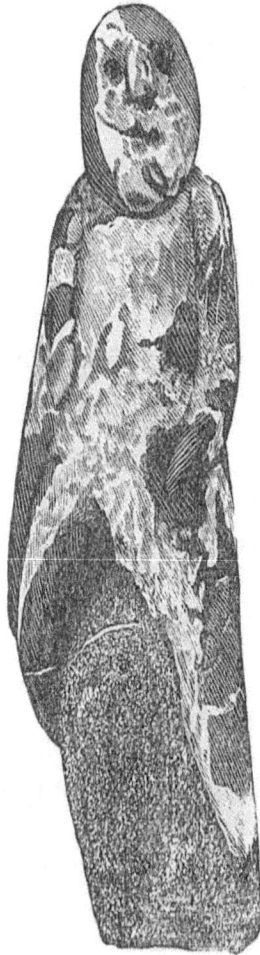

NOTES ON THE POEMS

I. THE KINGDOM OF HEAVEN IN THE HEART OF THE CHILD:
This poem was written at the request of my Mother to be recited at the vow renewal ceremony for her & my Father's 25th anniversary. When I wrote it I had the feeling I would be finding love. My own future wife, Audrey Cobb, happened to be catering the event & we shared our first kiss that evening in the same gazebo where the poem was read. It was my Mothers great wish to plan our wedding -she loved a good party. Though she did not get to see it, she was there in spirit.

II. WERID OLD AMERICA
This poem was inspired by my readings on Harry Smith in the book *American Magus, Harry Smith: A Modern Alchemist* edited by Paola Igliori. I had also seen an exhibition of Andy Warhol's screen tests at Cincinnati's Contemporary Arts Center. Harry Smith was the subject of one screen test. He was filmed making string figures. I felt a resonant transmission from watching Warhol's screen test of Harry. Around the same time I was reading Least Heat Moon's *Blue Highways*, which seemed very connected to Smith's idea of an "old weird America". This poem first appeared in *For a Better World: Poems & Drawings for Peace & Justice* (2012).

III. BLIND AT THE TILL
So much of life is spent trying to control our ultimate destiny. So much of popular Western magic over the past century has been aimed at manipulating the wheel of fate. Instead of trying to steer the wheel with white knuckles, we chose to relinquish the controls to some of the larger forces in the universe that can help guide us to shore?

IV. THE SPIDER
Set after William Blake's *The Tiger* this poem is an expression of some of the Arachnean magic I've explored in my dreamwork & in conjunctio with *The HermAphroditic ChaOrder of the Silver Dusk*. This first appeared in the second edition of Oryelle Defenestrate-Bascule's *emiT fo yrotSRIH feirB A*, & now in the third edition *Time, Fate & Spider Magic* from Avalonia Press.

V. **BLAZES IN THE BONE** This poem came to me after some visionary Underworld work I did on Halloween of 2013. That same October I had also done a series of *On the Way to the Peak of Normal* episodes on WAIF 88.3 FM focusing on the Faery, Underworld & Murder ballads from both the British Isles & Appalachia.

VI. **TAP ROOTS** This poem sprung from the idea of hibernating over the winter like the Great Bear of the North.

VII. **ROOTS CANAL** Ralph La Charity told me about the *Poems for Teeth* by Richard Loranger. With the aim to write poems both about roots & canals, I thought teeth could also be thrown in. As of yet I have thankfully not had a root canal. Playing with the imagery I came up with this sonnet.

VIII. **OKTOBERFEST, OHIO** My paternal Grandmother hailed from the German Catholic town of Fort Loramie, Ohio. My ancestors had come over from Germany to Cincinnati & helped dig the Miami & Erie Canal as well as the feeder Lake Loramie. By that time they had saved enough money to buy land & start farming. Minster is the town next door to Fort Loramie & I still have some kin there. The first weekend of October they hold an authentic Oktoberfest. My wife, Father, & Step-mom went up for the festivities one year & visited some gravesites as well, specifically my Great Grandmother Broering in the plot next to St. Michael's church.

IX. **DREAMER OF THE DARK** I consider Koizumi Yakumo or Patrick Lafcadio Hearn to be one of Cincinnati's great cultural ancestors. I wrote this ode after reading Paul Murray's excellent biography *Fantastic Journey: The Life & Literature of Lafcadio Hearn* on which I based the details of his life. This was first published in *For a Better World: Poems & Drawings for Peace & Justice* (2012).

X. **MILL CREEK BLUES** I live just a few blocks away from the Mill Creek, a stream that has been subject to much abuse since the arrival of industrialization. Maketewa is the Native American name for the stream which later became home to saw mills & meat canners. Biologist Stanley Hedeen writes in his definitive *The Mill Creek: An Unnatural History of an Urban Stream* " 'Maketewa' the Native American name for the stream meant 'he is black'. This title for a naturally clear creek might be taken as evidence for the Indians' gift of prophecy. Or, less imaginatively, the name 'Maketewa' may have referred to something other than the watercourse: heavy shadows in the stream bottomland, the rich soil in the floodplain, a memorable encounter in the valley with a runaway slave or a blackface-painted warrior or cassock-attired Jesuit missionary. However, the initial conjecture that 'Maketewa' embodies a prophetic vision of pollution is the only hypothesis that gains support from modern surveys of the dark stream." This was published first in *For a Better World: Poems & Drawings for Peace & Justice* (2015).

XI. **LEARNING TO SWIM** This was written as a kind of response to the title poem in Nancy Willard's collection *Swimming Lessons*.

XII. **THE COURTSHIP OF MA'AT** This was written after a visionary-ritual experience where an inner being stabbed me in the heart with a sword & then stuffed the wound with peacock feathers. To me this marked the beginning of rebalancing the scales in my life. The poem first appeared on the Horus-Maat Lodge website & also in the 2014 issue of *Aeqai*.

XII. **FLY FISHING WITH SUN RA** I was reading Paul Pines book of poems *Fishing from the Pole Star* in May of 2014. Paul has always been a jazz head & supporter of jazz musicians, running a club in New York & now an annual festival. At the time I was reading these fishing poems I became aware that it was also the centennial of the birth of Sun Ra, a longtime favorite of mine. I decided to write a fishing poem inspired by Paul, weaving in the cosmic keys of Sun Ra & his Arkestra. This poem appeared in the Autumn 2014 issue of *The Cafe Review*.

XIII. **UNDERWORLD GARAGE SALE** I ran across the two words "underworld garage" in Robert Lowell's poem *For the Union Dead*. I liked it, & it got me thinking about what an Underworld Garage Sale might be like. This one takes place in an alternate universe where my Uncle Dan, a Vietnam vet, became a garbage picker instead of a music aficionado. Dan Moore is a constant friend & was my stalwart companion at WAIF FM for over a decade of Radio Activity.

XIV. **C IS FOR MURDER** I wrote this poem after watching too many British crime dramas. Some were cozy murder mysteries, some more serious. I had also just finished reading Gertrude Stein's essay "Why I Like Detective Stories" (collected in *How Writing Is Written*). I especially liked her notion that mysteries are relaxing to read because the main character is dead & therefore you don't have to worry about what happens to them.

XV. **CAIN MARKS** Around the time this was written I had a series of synchronicities surrounding the figure of Cain, as the first vegetarian, founder of cities, & original outcast. This poem first appeared in the Aurore Press chapbook anthology *Unprofessional*.

XVI. **GASAHOL** Fossil fuel addiction is another form of substance abuse.

XVII. **AFTER THE AFTER PARTY** This post-peak-oil-poem first appeared in *For a Better World: Poems & Drawings for Peace & Justice* (2012).

XVIII. **A SKETCH OF THEE HELLSCAPE** Originally published in *For a Better World: Poems & Drawings for Peace & Justice* (2006).

XIX. **HOW TO BECOME A CONSPIRACY THEORIST** Riding the bus home one day with Mike Metz, a co-worker at the Public Library, he regaled me with the story of how someone had asked him the reference question "How do you become a conspiracy theorist?" Though there as of yet no *Conspiracy Theories for Dummies* type books this poem was my off the cuff response to that question & is dedicated to Mike.

XX. **THE CITY IS A DREAM** A nightscape psychogeography of the Queen City. This was first printed in spool number four of *Silk Milk Magi-Zain* published by Inspiral Multimedia Press.

XXI. **LUCIFERINS** Luciferin (from the Latin lucifer, "light-bringer") is a generic term for the light-emitting compound found in organisms that generate bioluminescence. In this case I was contemplating those types that live in the underwater caverns of the deep.

XXII. **PSYCHOACOUSTIC MEDICINE** A collage of musical references -band names, album & song titles, & lyrics- written at the end of my 13 year stint on community radio. An earlier version of this was read on the final broadcast of the program *On the Way to the Peak of Normal.*

XXIII. **WHAT MAGIC IS** A contemplation of the art & craft.

XXIV. **THE ELECTRIC SNAKE BOOGY** This bit of prose was written in a kundalini fever after I had a dream where I was bit by a cobra snake at the bottom of my spine. It first appeared in the Aurore Press chapbook *Unprofessional.*

XXV. **FUNERAL FOR A PUNK ROCK JACKET** This was written after I threw away a punk rock jacket I had made around age fifteen from a German Army coat. I was standing at the North Gate in a ritual when I heard the garbage truck come & take the coat away. It was then that the Great Bear of the North wrapped me in a coat made of her fur. Sometimes old skins have to be shed in order to make room for new ones.

XXVI. **THE RIVER STYX, REVISITED** Written after Mary Oliver's poem & collection *The River Styx, Ohio.* The River Styx is in Medina County, Ohio.

XXVII. **GOOSE SHIT RADIATOR** Free verse in honor of the birds made from a mish mash of memory.

XXVIII. **DIONYSIAN WINE** Written after a dream of the Silver Dusk.

XXIX. **THE HAND RETURNS TO IT'S WORK** A modest attempt at healing the cultural split between Dionysian & Appollonian approaches to life & art.

XXX. **UNDERGROUND RIVERS** Over the course of several years in my dreams I visited a number of different underground rivers, streams, sewers, tunnels, watercourses. That work now springs forth in this book, & elsewhere.

ABOUT THE POET

Justin Patrick Moore is thus far a lifelong resident of the Miami Valley Watershed where he dwells with his wife & family. A library cleric, he also worked in community radio for around thirteen years & has been an itinerant experimental sound maker in the Astral Surf Gypsies, Neato Torpedo & The Hollow Crown. His prose work has been published in *Flurb, Abraxas* & *Witches & Pagans Magazine.* Justin blogs on the subjects of dreams, magic, art & culture at the end of the industrial age at sothismedias.com.

Oneiric Imprint

Oneiric Imprint exists to publish & manifest the dreamed book; to prescribe readers medicine for the soul; to defend & uphold the Word; to spread the work of visionaries who have labored in the inner scriptorium. Our publishing philosophy rests at the crossroads of tradition & innovation, our projects incubated in the liminal margins of waking & sleep. Oneiric Imprint seeks to merge the weave of text with the Book of Nature.

Peregrinatio In Stabilitate

Our other titles include:

High Gravity *Werewolves, Ghosts, & Magick Most Black by PLATONIC ONE as channeled by Ken Henson*

The Dyslexicon *Journal of Hypnagoic Revelations, Flotsam, Jetsam & Recalcitrant Debris*
Issue 8, 2013: Dreams, Time Travel & Spiders

http://www.sothismedias.com/oneiric-imprint/